W9-CBU-646

August 2006
Love, Wes & Benita

THE PAINTED GARDEN
A year in words and watercolours
by Mary Woodin

COURAGE
BOOKS

© 2005 by Mary Woodin
All rights reserved under the Pan-American and International Copyright Conventions
Printed in China

This book may not be reproduced in whole or in part, in any form or by any means, electronic or mechanical, including photocopying, recording, or by any information storage and retrieval system now known or hereafter invented, without written permission from the publisher.

9   8   7   6   5   4   3   2   1
Digit on the right indicates the number of this printing

Library of Congress Control Number: 2004110025

ISBN 0-7624-2354-4
Art direction by Ken Newbaker
Cover design by Gwen Galeone
Edited by Caroline Tiger

This book may be ordered by mail from the publisher.
But try your bookstore first!

Published by Courage Books, an imprint of
Running Press Book Publishers
125 South Twenty-second Street
Philadelphia, Pennsylvania 19103-4399

Visit us on the web!
www.runningpress.com

For my family

Contents

July.

the herb garden

in midsummer

August. Keeping the garden in trim.

September. Warm tones of late summer

October. First leaves are turning

November.

December.

Berries and birdsong.

A celebration of evergreens

"Without an inborn love of natural beauty, no one will ever care enough about drawing to persevere."

MRS C.W. EARLE 1887

Foreword.

The idea for this book arose out of my two greatest passions — it is an artist's and a gardener's journal. I have spent a glorious year, paintbrush in one hand, trowel in the other, recording the comings and goings in my garden. from bulbs and blossom, to birds and a baby!

I live in Blackheath, a delightfully leafy suburb of London, with my husband Andrew, daughter Saskia and baby Reuben, who entered the scene halfway through this year.

In the 1830s our georgian house was surrounded by fourteen acres of hayfields, green lawns and a boating lake. Sadly no more. Now we content ourselves with being surrounded by birdsong and enough garden to grow my favourite flowers.

I studied at the Royal College of Art, London, and flower painting was a discipline that was instilled in me early on. All the paintings in this journal were done in watercolour, and most of them outside in the garden.

The starting point for my garden was to grow the flowers I love to paint — irises, roses, cottage garden favourites — scabious cosmos, sweet-peas. Each plant comes with its own history —

some I've nurtured lovingly from seed. Rarely can I resist a
purchase at the nursery of a memorable garden, and I can always
find a space for orphans when my mother has been dividing her
perennials. And so my garden grows.

"If you would be happy for a week, take a wife,
If you would be happy for a month, kill your pig,
But if you would be happy all your life — plant a garden."

CHINESE PROVERB

"To me the meanest flower that blows can give
Thoughts that do often lie too deep for tears."
WORDSWORTH

January.

prunus

forsythia

Japanese cherry

cornus

winter
jasmine

flowering currant

salix

birch

The fragile first petals
on the prunus

Iris Reticulata

anemone blanda
in the woodland
garden.

periwinkle - sorcerer's violet

4th Jan. Gales and
lashing rain. First disaster
of the new year - my rose obelisk
has been reduced to a tangle of sticks.
"Riding on the crest of a wave that tries to submerge us is
one of the phases of our existence that makes life most
satisfactory and worth living, and it is the secret of all progress.
If gardening were easy, even under favourable circumstances,
we should none of us care to do it." MRS C.W. EARLE. POT-POURRI FROM A
SURREY GARDEN 1887.

9 th Jan.
A mild day with
sunny spells. The
blue-tits are pirouetting in
the forsythia. I put up some
feeders for them, but have
failed in my attempts to
make them squirrel proof.
The blackbirds and thrushes
swoop down on the apple
peelings left out for them.
13 th Jan. St Hilary's Day —
the coldest day of the year.
The camellia buds are already
fat and flushed with pink.

Blue Tit

Great Tit.

"A Gard'ner's work is never at an end; it begins with the Year and continues to the next." JOHN EVELYN
THE GARD'NER'S ALMANAC 1664

Primula Gold Lace

19th January. We're enjoying sunny but cold days with early morning frosts. Covered new shoots on the perennials with bracken to deter Jack Frost's icy fingers. The japonica quince is smothered with goblets of deep coral. Pale blue dwarf irises spread wide their papery tongues of pastel colour. Primulas parade their jewels of scarlet and purple.

hyacinth daffodil crocus tulip

28th Jan. A muted grey day with mist-like rain that lingers on the air.

Cyclamen hederifolium

Pinks blooming on the rockery

Lonicera fragrantissima

A short walk around the garden gives a thrill almost more profound than the generosity of summer. Each twig closely observed is filled with anticipation. Tiny pink buds on the prunus, knobbly curves on the cherry and apple, the smooth red bark of the dogwoods.

flowering currant.

February.

"Bees come out of their hives, the partridge begins to pair, the blackbird whistles and the field and woodlarks sing."

J.C. LOUDON 1882 ENCYCLOPAEDIA OF GARDENING.

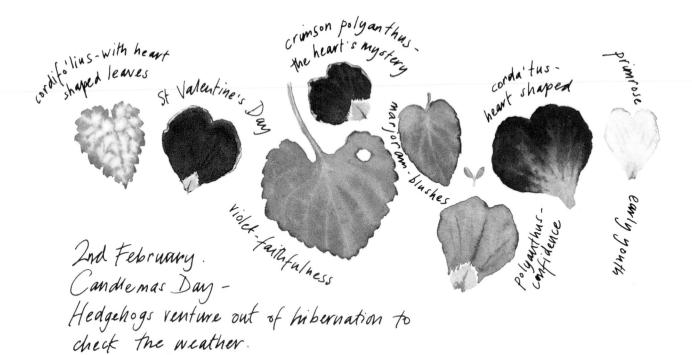

cordifolius - with heart shaped leaves

St Valentine's Day

crimson polyanthus - the heart's mystery

marjoram - blushes

corda'tus - heart shaped

primrose

violet - faithfulness

polyanthus - confidence

early youth

2nd February.
Candlemas Day -
- Hedgehogs venture out of hibernation to
check the weather.
4th Feb. Very frosty but gloriously sunny. The first camellia
is out waving petticoats of candy pink. An incongruous colour I
always think, amidst the winter palette of yellow and
white. Aconites and snowdrops are out, and the rosemary
is peppered with smoky blue flowers.
10th Feb. The first buds on the flowering plum have opened
and look like large soft flakes of snow caught in mid-air.
14th Feb. St Valentine's day - The day when birds traditionally
choose their mate. All morning a couple of pairs of blue tits
and a pair of great tits have been paying visits, in turn
with the squirrels, to my bird feeder.

Crocus - Gipsy Girl

Grape hyacinth

Hyacinth Blue Princess

18th Feb. An unusually warm weekend has coaxed the garden into bloom - the flowering plum is smothered in white blossom. The crocuses which have stood tightly budded for several days, flaunt their petals in the sun. Plant them near lavender to stop the birds pecking the petals.

24th St Matthias's Day

'St Mathee sends
The sap up the tree.'

27th February.
The forsythia buds that the birds
haven't stripped are now showing
quite yellow, and the wintersweet
is out around the pond.
The rhubarb is pushing its first
crumpled leaves through the strawy
manure that covers it. Place dark
heavy pots over, to force the tender
pink shoots.
28th Feb. Dug out a new south —
facing border in the back garden.
Picked out bucketfuls of stones to use
as drainage at the bottom of pots.
Pruned the roses. The pink climber
has not stopped flowering all winter.

forcing rhubarb.

"Crocuses – Protect from birds by running a small piece of white thread or string along, six inches above the plants, thin, and almost invisible; the bird does not see it till it alights for a feast, and before proceeding to make a meal of the budding Crocus it looks up, sees the string, pipes out danger, and away it goes, and familiarity with the thread does not breed indifference, for the same process is repeated again and again, to the safety of the Crocuses; coloured string is of no use as a preventive."

THE ILLUSTRATED GUIDE FOR AMATEURS
DANIELS BROS. 1876

H.E.R.B.S

CHIVES
Allium schoenoprasum

12" - 15" height
prefers a
bright sunny
position
and moist
soil

TOMATO
GARDENERS
DELIGHT

MARJORAM
(POT)

Origanum onites

Ordinary soil
Soft green leaves
purple
flowers late summer

Culinary uses

use leaves
in
stuffings with
meats
or vegetables.

HARDY PERENNIAL
LUPIN
RUSSELL MIXED

SUN OR
PARTIAL
SHADE

MARCH

HELXINE
BABY'S TEARS

Keep soil moist

Fragaria
PINK PANDA

Ideal for border, hanging
Baskets and containers

Clematis
Elsa Späth

" IN MARCH AND APRILL, FROM MORNING TO NIGHT,
IN SOWING AND SETTING GOOD HUSWIVES DELIGHT. "
THOMAS TUSSER . FIVE HUNDRED POINTS OF GOOD HUSBANDRIE 1573.

cottage garden mix

Plant your seeds in a row

 1. for the pheasant

 1. for the crow

 1. to rot and

 1. to grow   anon

cosmos

love in a mist

cornflower

nasturtium

sweet pea

hollyhock

aquilegia

knautia

scabiosa

candytuft

Trowel

Garden line for nice straight rows

rake the soil to a fine tilth

Dibber

2"   4"   6"   8"

carrot   cress   cauliflower   cabbage   brussels   leek   lettuce   radish   beetroot   parsnip   pea   courgette   french bean   runner bean

March 6th. Checked seed packets for sowing times. Sowed aquilegia knautia and viola.

"March 6. 1771. Monticello. Sowed a patch of peas after steeping them in water for 24 hours.

7. rain, snow and hail with an Easterly wind for 4 days.

25. Peas up.

May 26. The greatest flood ever known in Virginia.

30. Peas of Mar 6 come to table." JEFFERSON'S GARDEN BOOK 1771

Plant marigolds with potatoes to keep pests at bay, and sweetpeas amongst beans to increase yield. To ensure germination of melon seeds, warm them before sowing —

"March 15. 1755. Carry'd Mr. Garnier's Canteleupe-seed..in my breeches pocket 6 or 8 weeks." GILBERT WHITE

VEGETABLE SEEDS

RADISH
SCARLET WHITE-TIPPED EARLY

VEGETABLE SEEDS

CAULIFLOWER
PILGRIM (late April - May) 50 seeds

PEA - RONDO

Height 25-30 in   200 seeds

VEGETABLE SEEDS

CARROT
FLY AWAY   500 seeds

20th March. The magpies and rooks, of which we have far too many in the garden, are busy pulling moss from the lawn for their nests.

"We have a tradition or, if you will a superstition, in this part of the world, that rooks always begin to build on the first Sunday in March." HENRY A. BRIGHT. A YEAR IN A LANCASHIRE GARDEN 1879

21st. The ground is still damp - I spent a happy afternoon weeding!

"Here remember, that you never take in hand or begin the weeding of your beds, before the earth be made soft, through the store of rain falling a day or two before." THOMAS HYLL THE GARDENER'S LABYRINTH 1590

23rd The violets are out in full now, deep, velvety and fragrant. Their flowers are fairly short-lived, but I value them almost as much for their abundant heart-shaped leaves which provide good ground cover for shady corners, all year round. Growing through them, the compact heads of grape hyacinths nod silently, "as if a cluster of grapes and a hive of honey had been distilled and compressed together into one small boss of celled and beaded blue" RUSKIN.

April.

"Is any moment of the year more delightful than the present? What there is wanting in glow of colour is more than made up for in fullness of interest. Each day some well-known, long remembered plant bursts into blossom."

HENRY A. BRIGHT. A YEAR IN A LANCASHIRE GARDEN 1879

Japanese Cherry

"In Aprill, The Double
white Violet, The Wall-flower;
The Stock-Gilly-Flower;
The Couslip;
Flower-Delices;
and Lilies
of all Natures;
Rose-mary
Flowers; The
Tulippa; The
Double Piony;
The Pale Daffadill;
The French Honny-
Suckle; The Cherry-
Tree in Blossome."
FRANCIS BACON 1598

The first spring blown anemone
she in his doublet wove,
to keep him safe from pestillence
wherever he should rove.
TRAD RHYME

leather gauntlets

12th April

Blustery sunny day.
Secure clematis, tie
in new shoots around
rose arch. Wallflowers
are out.
"Most operations may be
performed with common
gloves. Thus, no gardener
need have hands like
bear's paws"

cotton
gloves

J.C. LOUDON. ENCYCLOPAEDIA
OF GARDENING 1871

For if in your house a man shoulders a spade,
for you and your kinsfolk a grave is half-made.

"Beware of all enterprises that require new clothes"
THOREAU 1854

Recipe for waterproofing boots before
the invention of Wellingtons –
1 pint boiled linseed oil
½ lb mutton suet
4oz resin
6oz clean beeswax.
melt, mix and brush, whilst still
warm, onto dry leather boots or shoes.

Espalier
Laxton Fortune

Apple - Espalier Spartan

James
Grieve

Malus
Red Glow

Royalty

Apricot Fan Moorpark

Simco

Morello
Cherry

Nectarine Fan
Pineapple

Fig-Fan

Apple

Ballerina bolero

"The reign of pink is inaugurated in the garden with the festival of the blossoms. We have the full-costumed Peach trees, the twisted, rose-wrapped branches of the Crab apples and many exquisite forms of pink double flowered Japanese Cherries and Plums."

LOUISE BEEBE WILDER
COLOUR IN MY GARDEN
1927

The higher the plum
the riper the plum

Plant pears for
your heirs

If apples bloom in March
for fruit you may search

my father's quince tree

April 26th.
Cherry, apple, pear, nectarine, apricot - I spent a lovely sunny day painting in a favourite orchard, surrounded by every shade of pink my palette could contrive. From the softest peachy pink on the bud of 'bolero', to the purple madder of malus 'royalty'.

"Dig the ground three spits deep —
that is, the depth of three spades —
and put in everything you can
that is good : well-rotted farm-
manure, the emptying of cesspools,
butcher's offal, dead animals,
anything to enrich the soil for a
long time."

MRS C.W. EARLE ~ ON PLANTING
ASPARAGUS. "POT-POURRI FROM A SURREY GARDEN" 1887

pea

broad bean

radish

"Carrets are good to be eaten with saltfish. Therefore sowe Carrets
in your Gardens, and humbly praise God for them, as for a
singular and great blessing; Admit if it should please God that
any City or towne should be besieged with the Enemy, what
better provision for the greatest number of people can bee, then
every garden to be sufficiently planted with Carrets?"

RICHARD GARDINER 1603

May

"Man has availed himself of the great laws of evolution in mightier matters than the Iris, but in no theatre of his unsleeping efforts has he created purer beauty or wakened for flower lovers a truer joy than among the bearded Irises."

EDEN PHILLPOTT
COUNTRY LIFE MAGAZINE 1917

"For his excellent beautie and rarietie deserveth first place." JOHN PARKINSON 1627 (ON THE IRIS)

1st May. If I had to choose one favourite flower it would be the iris. They will very soon be out - already their tightly parceled petals are yearning to be unwrapped. The first rose is out, the sage is in flower and alive with bees. The ceanothus is a glorious swathe of powder blue, but the slugs are munching the poppies.

8th May. The week has ended with a flourish — the irises are out! The weather is still unfavourably cold, which means numb fingers and several pairs of socks whilst I'm out painting. I want to capture their stance, sometimes standing tall, other times bowing under the weight of heavy blooms. The velvety depth of their petals with their translucent ruffled edges. Colours are never harsh - purple fades to blue, yellow to gold, orange to russet. The way the bud opens, the papery casing peeling away, and the way, all too soon, those princely petals curl in on themselves to die.

The fairest flowers soonest fade TRAD. SAYING

Jobs aside. May is a wonderful time for making garden
visits to enjoy the bounty of the month.

23rd May. The scrolled iron gate gives a melodic clang as we
turn the rusty handle and step into the courtyard, the
air heavy with the perfume of roses. Noisettes, Sweet briars,
Hybrid Teas, Chinas. An old fashioned white climber with
great glorious blooms scrambles over centuries of red brick.
Creamy nasturtiums tangle at it's feet. Two stone dogs
gaze faithfully on - the lichen of ages colouring their backs.
A narrow gravel path leads along the golden walk -
a shimmering avenue of apricot roses, lemony lupins
and orange lilies. Down worn steps, past pillars and
urns, at each turn the senses are besieged - a shower
of mauve clematis, a curtain of white foxgloves, lupins
painted in every shade of pink.

In the kitchen garden, the rhythmic scraping of a hoe echoes off the enclosing walls. Peach leaves curl against south facing brick.

feverfew

silvery sage

golden leaved marjoram.

tiny variegated Thyme

chives bordering the rhubarb

Behind the Victorian greenhouse, tulip bulbs dry in the midday sun. Inside, garlands of scarlet geraniums twist and twirl.

Sweet pea wigwams at the corners of the vegetable plot.

1. Captain Scott
2. Southampton.
3. Blue Triumph
4. Jasmine Kalm
5 Xenia Field

"This little space which scented box encloses
Is blue with lupins and is sweet with thyme
My garden all is overblown with roses,
My spirit is all overblown with rhyme,
As like a drunken honeybee I waver
From house to garden and again to house,
And undetermined which delight to favour,
On verse and rose alternately carouse."

VITA SACKVILLE-WEST 1917

June

"The rose doth deserve the chiefest place amongst all flowers whatsoever; being not only esteemed for its beauty, virtues and fragrant and odoriferous smell but also because it is the honour and ornament of our English sceptre."

GERARD. HERBAL 1597

English Rose Redcoat.

Rosa Essex

Rosa Suffolk

Rosa Kent

Rosa Surrey

miniature roses

June 1st. Roses are one of the most challenging flowers to paint - to capture at once the depth, the softness, the layers of interwoven petals, the fragility of white or the richness of red.

"There should be beds of roses, banks of roses, bowers of roses, hedges of roses, edgings of roses, baskets of roses, vistas and alleys of roses."

REVD. SAMUEL REYNOLDS HOLE. A BOOK ABOUT ROSES 1869

Fragaria vesca

3rd June. The strawberries
are ripe. Legend has it, the
first strawberry should be
given to the birds, but not
until I've painted it.
Anyway, my daughter Saskia

is much quicker off the mark than the birds when it comes to red strawberries. My mother arrived with a basketful of redcurrants from her garden. Made redcurrant and mint jelly – add a handful of fresh mint to the redcurrants whilst cooking.

4th June.
Picked herbs for drying – in the morning once the dew had evaporated.

made flavoured vinegars

THYME

RASPBERRY

BAY

REDCURRANT

Weigela

lituiflo'rus –
trumpet-flowered

11th   Bluebells – "in falls of sky colour washing
the brows and slacks of the ground
with vein-blue."
GERARD MANLEY HOPKINS

pen'dulus –
hanging down

aequipet'alus –
equal petaled

campannla'ria –
bell shaped

odora'tus – fragrant.

Lily-of-the-valley

Heuchera

Clematis
montana

Elsa Späth

"Rose, rose and clematis,
Trail and twine and
clasp and kiss."
ALFRED, LORD TENNYSON.

rubrican'lis –
red-
stemmed

"with five little hollowe hornes,
as it were hanging foorth,
with small leaves standing
upright of the shape of
little birds." GERARD.

Aquilegia vulgaris - Columbine
or . . . .
 Granny's bonnet,
  Lady's slippers,
 Doves in the Ark,
  Fool's cap '
   Hen and chickens.

"There are few businesses which may not be learned in much less time than that of a gardener can possibly be."

J. C. LOUDON

"I wish I could in any words paint the hues of these splendid Delphiniums; such shades of melting blue, some light, others dark, some like the summer heaven, and dashed across their pale azure wings with delicious rose."

CELIA THAXTER. AN ISLAND GARDEN 1894

iris   montbretia

grammy's bonnet

geranium

old fashioned pinks

nemesia

foxgloves

lychnis

June 28th

A day out. A summery day - blue skies and warm sunshine. The grass is still a little damp as I sit down to paint - it smells so sweet as it dries. Borders of mixed perennials are woven with colour and texture. Tall spires of kniphofia tilt over sweeps of montbretia. Cushion heads of verbena cast a purple haze, freckled with pale pink geranium. The clip of secateurs and the swish of a rake give away the gardener's pursuits among the azaleas.

"A man cannot be a good gardener, unless he be thoughtful, steady, and industrious: posessing a superior degree of sobriety and moral excellence, as well as genius and knowledge adapted to his business. He should be modest in his manners and opinion." J.C. LOUDON
ENCYCLOPAEDIA OF GARDENING 1871

July

"I know nothing so pleasant as to sit there on a summer afternoon, with the western sun flickering through the great elder-tree, and lighting up our gay parterres, where flowers and flowering shrubs are set as thick as grass in a field, a wilderness of blossom, interwoven, intertwined, wreathy, garlandy, profuse beyond all profusion."

Mary Mitford
Our Village

8th July – Even in a garden already wallowing in colour, nature herself produces delightful surprises that supersede our best-laid plans. I found a pale blue iris amidst a cloud of faded pink geranium. One bird-sown cerise double poppy, papery feathered petals, new and crumpled.

It is the herb sacred to remembrance and therefore to friendship

Chives – Allium schoenoprasum recorded in China 4000 years ago

Rosemary – Rosmarinus officinalis

Nasturtium – Tropaeolum majus Originates from Peru – easy to grow in a sunny position

Lavender

10th July.
The sweet marjoram seems to be coming up all over the place in the herb garden – but I let it, because it has pretty pink flowers that attract the bees and butterflies, followed by purple seed heads in autumn.

'Lavender is almost wholly spent with us, for to perfume linnen, apparell, gloves and leather and the dryed flowers to comfort and dry up the moisture of a cold braine'
Parkinson
Garden of Pleasure

millstone at the entrance to the herb garden

salad burnet bruised leaves smell like cucumber. russian sage good for stuffing duck, goose and pork. golden marjoram feverfew featherfew, bachelor's buttons, daisy like yellow centred flower. fennel 'we use it to lay upon fish or to boyle it therewith and with divers other things, as also the seeds in bread and other things' Parkinson 1640. rue 'the juice thereof warmed in a pomegranate shell or rind and dropped into the ears helps the pains of them' Culpeper. Pink hyssop traditionally used to clean sacred places. evergreen bushy herb native to southern europe. wormwood very bitter herb grow near hen houses to deter lice. bistort snakeweed, broad oval leaves with heart shaped base. sweet cicely myrrhis odorata, botanic name derived from greek word for perfume. angelica should flower on the feast day of Archangel Michael. golden sage 'how can a man grow old who has sage in his garden' Chinese proverb. garden catmint attracts bees and cats! beware. rosemary spread linen to dry over a rosemary bush in the sun - the lasting fragrance will repel moths. alecost introduced to America by early settlers who used the fragrant leaves as bookmarks in their bibles. Lavender from the latin 'lavare' to wash, hang a bag of lavender flowers in the flow of water when filling a bath. valerian grow near vegetables to encourage growth. purple sage soothes the throat

when used in tea. thyme the garden time, to be placed nigh to Bee-hives (for the commodity of honey) Thomas Hyll 1590. white hyssop. pot marjoram ancient culinary herb named by the Greeks - 'joy-of-the-mountain' silver Thyme. narrow leaf sage spanish sage, good for teas chamomile tea for insomnia tansy good antiseptic properties marigold calendula believed to be always in flower on the first day of each month. welsh onion from China and Japan - white flowerhead strong flavoured cylindrical leaves. blue anise vervain supposed to have originated in Egypt from the 'tears of Isis' blue hyssop loved by bees and butterflies horehound heart shaped, hairy wrinkled leaves, high in vitamin C. Old man Southernwood or wormwood. Its ashes mixed in an ointment will promote the growth of a beard. Women would carry large bunches to church to ward off drowsiness. Lemon balm "An essence of Balm, given every morning will renew youth, strengthen the brain, relieve languishing nature and prevent baldness"
Loudon Dispensary 1696 french sorrel grows in mountainous districts, good for soups cotton lavender or santolina, yellow button like flowers. Place twigs amongst linen to keep the moths away Good King Henry or goosefoot. boil and eat like spinach. also called 'fat hen' after the habit in Germany of feeding it to poultry. lungwort or Jerusalem cowslip, spotted with white, resembling the appearance of lungs. chives chop and mix into the food of newly hatched turkeys.

15th July- Arrived back
from holiday intoxicated
with impressions of
gardens visited, to
find my garden
tangled with
colour

and vigour –
cornflower
potentilla, achillea
scabious, heuchera.
nigella, nasturtium,
viola, poppy, lychnis,
anemone japonica –
marked the best
blooms with coloured
thread as a reminder of which
seeds to collect later in the year.

" Never fail, as you go by, to record
what bush is to be moved, and
which retained, and which is
pretty, and which, on
consideration, is held
unworthy of too
prominent a
place "

Reginald Farrer
In a Yorkshire Garden
1909

30th July 6 P.M. I pause to put my feet up on
someone else's bench, a fine victorian affair with
small wheels at one end for easy manoeuvering.
Positioned at the moment to catch the last of
the evening sun. Past low lines of santolina and
trimmed lawn, the garden becomes delightfully
overgrown. Our legs are teased by broken stems as
we linger on the narrow gravel paths. Above the
scuffle of our feet on the

stones, I can hear
the leaves of the copper beech
whispering dryly to one another, and the hum of bees,
busy about the sedum. Still blooming, towering heads
of sunflowers in shades from coral to russet. A feathery
bank of cosmos—deep pink, paler and crisp white.
Sweet peas meander along the perimeter of the
vegetable patch. A wall of espalied pears, golden in the
evening sun, hang heavy in the sheltered warmth of
chiselled flint. Apples cluster around twisted boughs,
blackbirds and bees feast on those that have fallen already.

August.

"About the edges of the yellow corn,

And o'er the gardens grown somewhat outworn

The bees went hurrying to fill up their store;

The apple boughs bent over more and more;

With peach and apricot the garden wall

Was odorous, and the pear began to fall

From off the high tree with each freshening breeze."

WILLIAM MORRIS. "AUGUST"   EARTHLY PARADISE   1868-1870

2nd August. Japanese anemones billow in skirts of pink and white, sweetly scented honeysuckle catches the breeze.

"Of all the months in the year this is the one in which the keenest amateur can best afford to leave home, and if I do not go away, it is the one I can best spare to my gardener for his holiday."

MRS C. W. EARLE
POT-POURRI FROM A SURREY GARDEN 1887

A bit of a lull in the garden — an opportune time to give birth!
7th August. Reuben Charles entered the world safely in the midday heat. He has quickly become accustomed to being my garden companion — his pram neatly balancing my drawing board, sketching stool, and jam-jars for water. Parked under a tree he happily applies himself to the subtleties of cedar, oak or ash. Or sleeps.

August 20th

A garden visit - Along blackberry lanes, mixed beech hedges,
old man's beard and bracken. Heavy ripe elderberry heads.
A garden enclosed, an old brick wall, pink and grey,
spotted white with lichen, topped with moss.
An edwardian rockery on a sunny slope - creeping with
Fragaria, scented stocks, burgundy and yellow violas.
Dried marjoram heads, crisp purple brown.
A garden of surprises. An immaculate green croquet
lawn, enveloped by clipped yew, surveyed by two
topiary peacocks. Four wirey lurchers lope nose to tail
through a gateway, ash grey, white, brown and
sandy grey, long claws scrape across the flagstones.
Late summer colour - cosmos, penstemon, cornflower,
and purple asters. Newly planted limes create

an avenue down to a Doric temple. A scarecrow, straw hands and spotted necktie watches over ripe tomatoes. A garden of sounds - droplets from a fountain patter down on the creamy cups of a water lily. Black and white bantams scratch the earth and a peacock lets out a screech from the herbaceous border. A gentle breeze slips through the needles of an ancient cedar - its arms spread wide over the main lawn.

"There is nothing much more difficult to do in outdoor gardening than to plant a mixed border well, and to keep it in beauty through the summer."

GERTRUDE JEKYLL

22nd August. There's no break in the hot dry weather, which means the garden needs regular attention to keep it looking good. As gaps appear in the borders I pop in the odd well-chosen bedding plant to eke out the season. Begonia sempeflorens, with its rusty leaves and showers of white flowers, thrives in the shade of the cistus. A row of pinks spill their spidery limbs over the path. Nicotiana (Havanna Apple Blossom) near the house gives off its sweetest perfume in the evening. Terracotta pots overflow with double deep red geraniums.

23rd August. It's not dark until 10 pm. The warm

evenings are a soothing time – away from the midday
heat, to wander, pockets heavy with twine and secateurs,
snipping dead heads, propping up weary stalks, until
darkness obscures all sensible activity. Fading rose
petals catch the moonlight as they fall.
"No evening scents, I think, have the fascination of
the delicate fragrance of the evening primroses,
especially that of the commonist variety. Those pale
moons irradiate the twilight with their sweet
elusive perfumes. "
ELEANOUR SINCLAIR ROHDE.
THE SCENTED GARDEN

ageratum Blue champion

alyssum Gold

Easter bonnet

lobelia

Cambridge blue

String of pearls

Impatiens safari

orange star

begonia sypeflorens
Ambassador

tempo

Hanna King

Gold variegated

sage

pyrethrum

golden moss

Purpurea

Clary Sage

23rd.
Collected flowers for drying — rosebuds, achillea, larkspur,
hydrangea, nigella seed-pods. Hang upside down in
bunches in a dry dark room.

August 24th. St Bartholomew's Day.
St Bartholomew brings
the cold dew

Nigella damascena,
leave seed pods to self
sow for next year.

plumbago

sow more blue cornflowers next year

Buddlea to
attract the
butterflies.
Variegated
with deep
purple
flowers.

the cheery face of the viola

do not plant so
many nasturtiums
next year.

fragile angels choir poppy

too many weeds

saxifrage hiding around

the corner

Anemone
japonica
prefers
partial
shade

Lobelia
Queen Victoria

lovely evening scent
deep crimson, white and
lime green.

give the lupins a
dose of soapy water
to get rid of the slugs.

silvery
lamium
leaves for
dark
corners.

September

" For those who have not got very good
memories for the names of plants, I
strongly recommend them if they can draw
to make a little coloured sketch, however
small on the page of a gardening book next
the name of the plant. This will be found
a great help to the memory."

Mrs C. W. Earle
Pot-Pourri from a Surrey Garden.
1887.

elderberry

Wild strawberry

Rosa rugosa

Fragaria pink panda

9th September - collected seed pods

lupin

sweet pea

poppy

delphinium

love in a mist

scabious

hemerocalis

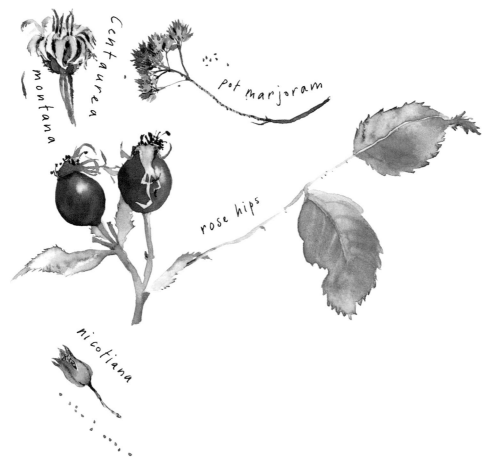

Centaurea montana

pot marjoram

rose hips

nicotiana

10th September – Jobs to be done.....

- tie in new shoots around rose arch while they're still supple.

- take cuttings of non-hardy plants for overwintering – osteospermum, lantana, geranium – leave the geranium cuttings on the potting bench to wilt overnight, they'll strike much better.

14th – Nutting day – the devil will hold the branches down whilst you harvest the nuts.

September 12th. Digging in the garden, making space for winter pansies, I unearthed a worm that had tied itself in a knot. I admit I was too squeamish to attempt to unravel it, and left it to its crooked path.

FLOWER SEEDS.

PANSY
GIANT
MIXED

AVERAGE
CONTENTS
100 SEEDS

"There are few things to be done in a garden which do not require a dexterity in operation, and a nicety in hitting the proper season for doing it."
Loudon. Encyclopaedia of Gardening 1871.

gold ochre
persian red
cobalt violet rose
cadmium yellow
burnt umber
french ochre
raw sepia
payne's gray

14th. A breezy day
but beautifully warm. The
soft billowing colours of summer
are giving way to autumn. Silver
grey and dusty brown, alchemilla
heads turned burnt sienna.
Santolina, lavender and lamb's
ears - grey green, brushed

with tall brown spires
of salvia. Michaelmas
daisies (wild asters)
"a symphony in purple,
the colour of the organ
peal are they" Martha
Flint. Golden rod - according
to legend grows on the site of
buried treasure - arches its
feathery heads over the back
of the border, while deep
yellow rudbeckias light up the
front. "The sun has shone on
the earth, and the golden
rod is his fruit" Thoreau
19th September -
Heard the woodpecker in
the tall ash.
21st September -
End of another week of
glorious sunshine. The
mornings start chilly and
the sun hardly rises above the

Nicotiana
Havana Appleblossom

Hemerocallis 'Stella d'Oro'

September Charm

Anemone japonica

Scabious

Pansy

Michaelmas Daisy

Catmint

Osteospermum 'Giles Gilbey'

Plumbago

Fuchsia
Madame
Cornelissen

23rd Sept.

tallest treetops, but it throws a lovely gentle light which doesn't bleach out colours like the burning summer sun. The catmint, its flowers scorched and papery white all summer, now glows an almost luminous purple in the kind afternoon sun. The creamy white lantana flowerheads sing against their deep lush foliage. Growing through it, the dainty blue star-like flowers of the plumbago enjoy a new intensity.

22nd – Planted out wallflowers – blood red, a good flower early next year for butterflies. I keep digging up shiny brown horse chestnuts, newly tucked underground by the squirrels. The horse chestnut leaves are beginning to turn olive and amber.

25th. Still warm and muggy – no rain for ages. For the first time this autumn I have crunched freshly fallen leaves underfoot.

October

"Under the influence of all this loveliness,
almost I am persuaded to love autumn
best, and forget a lifelong allegiance
to the spring-time of the year. Such
infidelity could be
brought about by nothing
less than a month like this, so
wondrously, serenely beautiful".
11th October, 1899

E.V. BOYLE 'SYLVANA'S LETTERS TO AN UNKNOWN FRIEND'

3rd October. Warm sunshine continues daily - many plants are having a second flush of flowers.

6th October. Our wedding anniversary. Andrew presented me with a cockerel! A delightful life-size rusty iron one. His chosen domain is among the lupins outside the kitchen window. He has quickly become a favourite vantage point for my resident robin redbreast.

7th. Rain at last. Woke this morning to see the soil soaked to a bitter chocolate colour. Fine droplets hang heavy on the   many cobwebs.

Winter weather and women's thoughts often change.

The dimpled leaves of alchemilla mollis each
cradle a tiny glistening pool. The japanese
anemones sway as naked stalks and the cosmos
droop.

8th October. Rain and bluster all day. The
dramatic change in the weather is a timely
reminder to bring in all my tender plants
before the first frosts catch us unawares.

15th. Planting out some rooted lavender cuttings,
a young frog surprised and delighted me —
quite camouflaged under the mexican orange,

I readily supposed he was busy reducing my slug
population. My weeding companion – a bright eyed
robin followed me closely, enjoying the pickings from
the newly dug earth.
- Always carry a conker in your pocket when digging,
to prevent backache. ANON
17th October. A warmer day but still damp. A
flock of sparrows chattering noisily in the forsythia give
the garden such an air of excitement, I'm almost
inclined to forgive them for stripping the bush of buds
earlier in the year.
Split some perennials that had become overcrowded -
sedum, scabious, stachys, heuchera, and started
enlarging old beds to accomodate them.
"It is a very good plan, when you want to
cut a new bed or alter the shape of an old
one, to shuffle along the wet dewy grass on
an October morning – and this leaves a mark
which enables you very well to judge the size
shape and proportion before you begin to cut

sedum

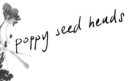

poppy seed heads

your beds out." MRS C W EARLE. POT-POURRI FROM A SURREY GARDEN
Saved the sedum flower heads (Autumn Joy) still
tinged with ruby red but by now quite dry, to combine
with jet black birch twigs and poppy seed heads for
Christmas wreaths.
18th October - St Luke's day - if it has been a poor
summer 'St Lukes little summer' will follow giving a few
days of good weather.
20th October - Traditionally the day to prepare mincemeat
for Christmas cooking - Chopped apple, raisins, currants,
sultanas, suet, brandy.
21st. The first leaves on the japanese cherries are flickering
yellow and orange. The flowering plum is fading from
deep purple to pinky red - the view through my studio windows
is becoming a completely new palette.
25th. First overnight frosts of the year. The begonias I
hadn't already brought indoors, to flower on the kitchen
windowsill, have been turned to a pulp.

birch twigs

raffia

elderberry

honeysuckle

honeysuckle

holly

 hawthorn

November

 Sorbus

yew

honeysuckle

pyracantha

bacciflava

" The garden is never dead ; growth is always going on and growth that can be seen, and seen with delight.

CANON H. ELLACOMBE 'IN MY VICARAGE GARDEN AND ELSEWHERE' 1901

November 18th. An extremely windy night followed by a pinky orange sunrise – and then heavy rain. The last few chrysanthemums are bowing sodden heads. Broken twigs lay scribbled over the lawn,

and the last few leaves have been tossed and discarded by the wind. The whole garden has assumed an air of melancholy.
"Sharpen and mend tools, gather oziers and hassell rods and make baskets in stormy weather"
1727

"One of the most disagreeable months...but he may console himself with the shortness of the day, and hail the approach of evenings when he may cast aside his wet dress and fortify his mind by converse with books."

J.C. Loudon Encyclopaedia of Gardening 1882

"footnote"

staked and tied vulnerable plants with strips cut from old stockings which will give in strong winds.

Found several toadstools growing on the old sycamore stump.

Butterfly Fairy Queen Wings Crown Princess of Prussia Imperial Purple Memories Orange Prince Painted Lady Scarlet striped Anniversary North Shore New Cupid Senator Venus

1   2   3   4   5   6   7   8   9   10   11   12   13   14

Autumn sown sweet peas have germinated.

November 19th

Noticed the first flower on the winter
jasmine — an invaluable shrub that will
thrive in the most unpromising of places and flower resolutely
throughout winter. I will be raiding it regularly along with
lonicera fragrantissima for indoor arrangements. The former
for it's cheerful yellow face, the latter for it's lemony fragrance.
A tall unidentified rose needs more support — so I set about
twisting sticks and twine to make an obelisk.

20th — St Edmund's Day — patron saint of gardeners and
farmers. Gathered a posy of flowers from the garden in his
honour.

"Set garlicke and pease
St Edmund to please"

Planted a few garlic
cloves near the roses to
repel aphids.

November 22nd All the leaves
have fallen off the forsythia
revealing a ragged sparrow's nest
entwined in its branches. Inside
an abandoned silver grey
snail shell looks strangely
egg like.

Cut some long flexible twigs
off the bush - wrapped them
around and around securing now
and again with raffia to make
a sphere for the top of
my rose obelisk.

"Even deep snow gives time for cleaning, thrashing and sorting

December

of seeds, preparing   stakes and pea-sticks,   tying mats,   sorting bulbs."

J.C. LOUDON

24th December.
Christmas Eve – Girls who want to conjure
up an image of their partner-to-be
should walk backwards, nine
times around a pear tree.

Christmas robin

chinese lantern

chilli pepper

kumquat

star fruit

lychee

chilli pepper

cranberries

chinese lantern

December 25th Christmas Day —
Unfortunately a rather wet and dreary day outside. When I looked out this
morning two fine lady hens had joined my cockerel in the lupins —
Thankyou Andrew!

"of statues, busts, pedestals, altars, urns and similar sculptures. Used
sparingly, they excite interest, often produce character and are always
individually beautiful." J. C. LOUDON. ENCYCLOPAEDIA OF GARDENING 1871.

Biographical notes:

E.V. Boyle 1825 – 1916 'Sylvana's letter to an unknown friend' 1900.
Wrote and illustrated books about the garden she
restored at Huntercombe Manor, Buckinghamshire.

Henry Arthur Bright. 1830 – 1884. 'A year in a Lancashire garden' 1879.
Partner in a shipping firm, also cultivated his
own garden in Lancashire, about which he
wrote and published his diaries.

Mrs C.W. Earle. 1836 – 1925. 'Pot-pourri from a Surrey garden' 1887.
Studied at South Kensington School of Art before
becoming a gardener, writer, wife and mother. She
established her own garden – 'Woodlands' in
Cobham, Surrey, and wrote extensively about it
and contemporary issues, in her diaries. She
published these, ignoring derisory comments from
her husband and they became immediate
bestsellers.

John Gerard 1545 – 1612. 'Herballe' 1597.
Elizabethan botanist. Published the first detailed
catalogue of plants in any single garden, based
on his own garden in Holborn, London.

Thomas Hyll. 1529 – ? 'The Gardener's Labyrinth' 1572. (Published
under the pseudonym. Didymus Mountain).

Thomas Hyll cont...d. First english-language popular gardening
manual to be published, which included
many new plants that were being introduced
into Elizabethan England by the explorers. Also
published books on astrology, cooking, popular
medicine, and psychology.

Thomas Jefferson. 1743-1826. 'Jefferson's Garden Book.'
American president and gardening enthusiast.
Wrote extensive diaries and correspondence
cataloguing his horticultural exploits.

J.C. Loudon. 1783-1843. 'Encyclopaedia of Gardening' 1871.
Horticultural editor, writer and traveller. His terraced
garden in Gravesend, Kent, could be classed as the
first public park. He also designed cemeteries,
and proposed a greenbelt for London.

Jane Loudon. 1807-1858. 'Instructions in Gardening
for Ladies' 1840.
Married J.C. Loudon in 1830. Travelled
with her husband and wrote popular
horticultural books as a
commercial exercise
to pay off his debts!

Mary Russell Mitford 1787-1855. 'Our Village' 1824-32
Lived with her father near Reading. England and wrote about gardening to support them both.

Vita Sackville-West (Hon) 1892-1962. A talented novelist and poet who also wrote a gardening column for the Observer newspaper for 25 years. She became best known however for her garden at Sissinghurst, Kent, which she created with her husband Harold Nicolson.

Henry David Thoreau 1817-1862 'The Writings of Henry David Thoreau'
American naturalist and writer who kept extensive journals of the habitat around his home at Walden Pond.

Louise Beebe Wilder 1878-1938 'Colour in my Garden.' 1927
Grew up in Baltimore and became one of America's best known and authoritative garden writers.